MAKE DOLLARS AND SENSE

A PRACTICAL GUIDE TO TAKING CONTROL OF YOUR LIFE AND FINANCES

LIISA BARNES

JayMedia
Publishing

Printed in the United States of America

ISBN: 978-1-957443-09-6 (paperback)
      978-1-957443-10-2 (ebook)

First printing, 2023

JayMedia Publishing
Laurel, MD 20708
www.publishing.jaymediagroup.net

Contents

Introduction

First, I would like to thank you for taking the time to read this book. I hope this book makes you think, cry, laugh, pray, get angry, and feel every other emotion. Above all else, I pray that this book makes you change. Change to the point of rethinking how you deal with money, and change how you see and commit to everyday life decisions. I sincerely hope this is the end of the road in financial mediocrity for you.

In reading this book, you will see yourself; you will see your family, you will see your friends, and you will also see your enemies. I say this because many of our mistakes with money didn't start with us. Most of our bad habits with money can be seen in the people around us, as well as in ourselves. It is almost like we all keep bumping into the same wall repeatedly, but nobody realizes it or acknowledges the wall. I intend to point out the wall, so we can stop running into it, tear it down, or at least go around it. I have no desire to bash anyone about their mistakes, but I have to call things out and get very specific because change requires discomfort. I cannot leave us (myself included) in our current state of disrepair. I want our eyes wide open, and I want us to see our financial and lifestyle folly and identify it as such.

I am not calling out repeated financial mishaps from generations past to simply get in or to stay in a low-paying job, just getting by or living for the weekend. When I talk about change, I am talking about getting your butt in gear and going after your dreams to the point of getting to know yourself again. I'm talking about setting up businesses, becoming an investor, living your best life, and teaching others to do the same. Those of us who were not born with a silver spoon in our mouths need to be getting in the game now. Get some precious metals, real estate, and other assets to pass down to future generations. You did not have control of the family you were given, but you can take care of the family that is not even alive yet and give them a better position in life. You should be the person that goes down in history for teaching your family sound financial principles and leaving multiple thriving businesses. Your actions will proclaim to your family your desire to leave a legacy for them and yourself.

Whether in a time of booming success or headed to the most devastating recession ever, the present time is all that we are promised. The present time is always the greatest time to get going and to make changes because it is within your control right now. So, be the generation that will change the game. To bring about the needed transformation, we have to restructure our thinking from just knowing or not knowing information to utilizing the information we have to create things and opportunities that have never existed for ourselves and our families before. We must make our dollars (increase our cash flow) and apply good sense (change our thinking).

This book is broken into daily lessons. Read one day at a time and do the reflection for that day. If you have to, read a day more than once; there is no rush. When you are done reading, think about what you have read, and let the day's message find you. As you go about your day, continue to visualize and take the necessary steps to bring the change you would like to see in your life. This book is designed to fit into a month's time frame, but please do not rush yourself. Take your time.

Don't be quick to judge others when you find them in the book, but take every measure to find yourself and address those concerns first. At the end, thank yourself for the new you. Be blessed, family.

Disclaimer

Day 1: Been Down This Road Before

In my early twenties, I found myself in credit card debt. I had no reason to have a credit card, but I wanted one badly. I thought I would be responsible once I had the card. In actuality, I needed to be responsible before I had it. In my 30's, I got other credit cards. Three others, to be exact. Two personal cards and one business card. I had about $40,000 burning a hole in my pocket. Initially, I was fine, but a few months later, I quit my job, looking to chase a dream without a plan. When my lack of a solid plan to finance my life revealed itself, I had to rely on those credit cards. I would take enough of a cash advance for all of my monthly expenses from one card. I would pay my bills (including the credit card from which I had just taken a cash advance) with a cash advance. I was living off of credit until it ran out. After that, I hid because I had no job and no more credit cards to rely on. I hid from all creditors for a few years. My credit report was taking major hits, but no job and money meant I couldn't pay what I owed. That was a very stressful situation to be in at the time. I couldn't even work out a deal because I didn't have a job. Then when I got a job, I made less money. Things in my life did not make sense for someone who worked hard to make her life make sense.

Going Forward

When I returned to the credit card game after about 10 or 15 years, I can honestly say I was wiser. I only used it to pay medical bills or when I needed a computer for my business. I never used more than 30% of the balance; spending at 30% or below shows the creditors and myself that I am responsible. My card allowed me no interest payments on all purchases for 12 months. When I did use it, I made sure that I paid everything off within that 12-month interest-free period.

This meant that I always paid more than the minimum to ensure I had the balance paid before the interest would kick in. By doing things this way, I was building my credit score, establishing a good history, being financially responsible for myself first, and saving money by not paying interest. Using my credit card in this manner allowed the card to be a tool for me, not a weapon I was using against myself. That makes sense, right?

Wealth Building Word: *Interest*

You can see interest as money paid to you for loaning your money. When you put your money into a bank savings or checking account, your money is being used by the entity holding your money. In return for allowing your money to be used by the bank, you are paid interest (a laughable amount, but we're not talking about that right now). Interest is usually paid at a scheduled time (for example, monthly) and a set rate when working with a bank. Banks also charge you interest when you borrow money from them.

Day 2: Do I Really Need This?

That is the question we should ask ourselves every time we purchase something. Like most people, I spend a great deal of money on things I don't need. Many people have shopping habits that drive them to spend, spend, spend. They think they need a new outfit or a new pair of shoes when they just got a new outfit and a new pair of shoes a few days before. Some of us may not buy clothes and shoes regularly, but we all have that habit that eats up our money. Mine is eating out. I love to eat out. I am single with no children, but my monthly food budget is larger than most families (so I'm told). I feel like my life is incomplete if I do not go out to eat somewhere. I feel lost if I go two or three days without eating food from a restaurant at least once. Your habit may not be buying shoes, clothes, or eating out, but everyone has that one thing they really do not need eating away at their opportunity to invest.

Going Forward

Ask yourself, *Do I really need this?*...before you make a purchase. If the answer is no, do not buy the item. I repeat...DO NOT BUY THE ITEM. You have to look at your money spent on foolishness as an opportunity lost. Effective investing takes time and money. You are wasting precious time if you never get your money into your investment account to work for you. If you need the item, buy it. By all means, take good care of yourself, but simultaneously keep your goals in mind.

Wealthy Building Word: *Dividend*

Companies pay their shareholders a percentage of the money they have left over after all the company's expenses are paid. This payment is called a dividend. Shareholders can receive their dividend payment as a payout to their personal account or as a check. Shareholders can also have their dividend payment reinvested back into the company's stock. When you reinvest the dividend payment you gain more shares of the company's stock which allows you to earn a higher percentage of the company's leftover money over time.

Day 3: Big Boss Aspirations

Who lied to you? Why do you continue the lie? Listen to your self-talk; you repeatedly tell yourself you do not deserve to be rich. You are saying *I do not deserve to be wealthy*. That is a lie. I know it is a lie because you have desires. You desire the most beautiful home. You would love to drive a fancy car. You want that designer bag. You love having all of the nicest things. You want to go into a store and get everything your heart desires. You want to go to your favorite restaurant as often as you like and order anything and everything you want on the menu. Face it... you have BIG BOSS aspirations, and that is okay.

There truly is nothing wrong with aspiring to live your best life. Money is not evil. Pursuing a better life for your family and yourself is a worthy goal. If more than enough luxuries come with you working smarter, that is okay. You deserve it. Just keep in mind that you have to be smart about your spending. Once your money is gone, it is gone if you do not take the time to learn to save and invest. On your new path and in your new mindset, you will prepare. You will not only live your best life, but you will do better than that. You will ensure that your name is great among your descendants for generations to come. You want the best for them; they will have the best because of you.

Going Forward

Speak to yourself. Speak to the self you desire to be. Speak to the inner you and bring it forward. Tell yourself how great you are. Tell yourself all that you deserve to have. Write it down, and most importantly, get busy working on it today. Don't let tomorrow catch you being the same person you were before reading this lesson. The purpose of a lesson is to learn something. When you learn something, put it into action immediately. Do better because you know better. Write your greatness down and tell yourself every day until you live it. I repeat, write your greatness down and tell yourself your story daily until you live it.

Wealth Building Word: *Will*

Since you will leave great riches and wealth to your family, you must leave a last will and testament. Your will is your way of communicating how you want your wealth managed and distributed to your loved ones. They will need to know how to take care of the fortune you left them. They will need to know that they can live off the interest from the money you invested during your lifetime without ever having to touch the principal. They can add to it, but they should never have to take away from your investments. That way, the wealth and riches you built for them will live on for many generations after you.

Day 4: The Purpose of Saving

I used to save to know there was money somewhere for me. I just thought having money was the right thing to do, so I saved when I could. Most of the time, my savings would dwindle to nothing. I mean, I could barely save $5. That is not an exaggeration. When I spent all my money, I felt so guilty and irresponsible. I felt like the sky would fall on me at times because I lacked preparedness for anything that might arise in my life. When the "rainy day" presented itself, would my life be ruined because I had wasted my hard-earned dollars? If a disaster were to strike, I needed to be ready.

I thought saving meant that I was living a good life and that things would improve over time. When I saw that no matter how much money I had in my account, I only received 1 or 2 pennies (literally) from my bank, I almost blew a fuse. How could they still just give me a penny when I had a few thousand dollars in the bank? What about interest? What about compound interest? I thought that was how the game was played...open an account, put your money in, and watch it grow. I thought the banks would play fair because I was leaving my money in the account and adding to it regularly. However, they did not change. I still got one little penny, no matter what.

Things had to change. I had heard of interest. I had also heard of compound interest. I had even heard of the stock market and knew that people put their money in there and received money back in addition to what they put in there. Yes, they got additional money back regularly in most cases. My dissatisfaction with 1 or 2 pennies, no matter my balance, led me on my journey to find my interest. My money sitting in my pocket, under a mattress, in a sock, buried in the woods, or in a regular savings account wasn't doing me any good. I needed to find a way to make my money grow while I slept, ate, vacationed, etc. I learned how to research and invest in solid companies. I took some of my money and invested it in my financial education. Then I applied my financial knowledge. I learned how to make my money work for me. Now I love to get notifications about the interest/dividend from my investments.

Going Forward

Find yourself an educational program that will teach you how to invest. You need to know how to look at financial statements and determine whether a company is rock solid or not. You need to learn that even after your best analysis, you may still pick a dud of a company, which is okay too. You need to know that the market will rise and fall to various extremes, but you must endure and not make rash decisions. You have to be informed about the markets. This is a process, but get started. Youtube is a great place to get started. Check out my channel @CatchGems where you will find a playlist named Markets Money Mindset. When you're really serious about learning the markets, reach out to me so we can talk and get you going in the right direction.

Wealth Building Word: *Cash*

Cash is just one way that we hold money or currency. In our society today, there are many alternatives to cash, so very few people carry cash. In some instances, cash is necessary. However, remember that your cash is not working for you while in your possession. When you put your cash into an investment of some type, expect it to grow. Only you can determine what you are willing to risk. The stock market is not for everyone. You may be more of a mutual fund or CD kind of person. All I am saying is to do more than save. Learn, invest, and expect your dollars to grow.

Day 5: Debt Doesn't Have to Be a Part of Your Life

There is nothing wrong with you if you are debt-free. Again, *you can be debt-free*, and it is okay. Debt is so prevalent in our society that people think it's normal. Something that robs and steals from your future shouldn't be accepted as a norm. That should never make sense to any of us. Debt should be looked at as a common problem but not as the collective normal. Increasing your debt is like setting up an issue and guaranteeing its growth in your present and future.

Say you like to buy cars, as many of us do, you put little to no money down, and your credit is shady. Before I say it, you already know your payments are sky-high. You're okay with it at first, and you tell yourself things like:

I got the car I wanted.

I can't see myself driving an old raggedy car.

I work hard for my money, so I can spend it how I want.

I'll never be rich unless somebody dies and leaves me something, so I might as well enjoy myself.

Don't look now, but 5, 6, 7, or even 8 years into the future, you will see that car payment is still there.

You may not have said any of the things I mentioned above. Maybe I'm the only person that thinks I should have instant gratification with no thought for the future. *NOT.* This issue doesn't even require deep research. Just stop, and look around you. It's harder for you to think of someone who has no debt than someone who isn't indebted to someone or something. Excessive and unnecessary debt is a problem. It just is. Accept the facts and move on to fix the problem. Debt on liabilities eats up your dollars and takes away your opportunity to make your money work in ways that benefit you.

Going Forward

Debt is common, but it is not normal. Just as pain in your body may be an everyday thing now, it is not normal. You remember how you felt when you could just get up and go without a care. You thought you would never get old, and nothing could hold you down, even when you were sick. You were free. You can feel that again. We can feel that again. We can get this debt sickness off of us and be free again. Pick a small debt, pay it off, or set up payment arrangements. Once the first debt is paid off, take that monthly payment amount you were paying on the first debt and put it towards the second debt, along with the monthly payment you were making on the second debt. Now you're making a larger payment on the second debt, but you're spending the same amount because the first debt is gone. Once the second debt is paid off, take all that money and put it toward a third debt. Keep going until everything is paid off. Once you execute your plan and have a handle on your debt, start investing your money. Find investments you are comfortable with, whether stocks, real estate, mutual funds, crypto, etc.

Wealth Building Word: *Asset Allocation*

Assets (real estate, precious metals, etc.) are financial instruments that you expect to provide a future increase in value when you invest in them. Allocation means putting something in a place or category that is separate from another place or category. In simple terms, asset allocation means putting your dollars into different investment categories. Common categories include stocks, bonds, mutual funds, and real estate.

Day 6: I Don't Want the Pie in the Sky

Some of us don't believe anyone needs a lot of money. They say they don't think they need a lot of money, but many of those people have a lot of debt. They owe everybody. They also have expensive habits. Yes, those same people like to party all the time. Regularly buying drinks and food for friends and family at bars and restaurants requires money. On top of that, your regular expenses also require money. You need as much money as you can get. I can't say it any other way; you absolutely need as much money as you can get to maintain your habits and do the things you enjoy doing.

Many people think they know the number of dollars that they want. They think of a certain number because they think there is a limit. There is no limit; the only limit is the boundary that you set for yourself.

When you hear billionaire wealth estimates, that is precisely what it is...an estimate. Truly wealthy people can't count all their money because they are making money from many different assets. Their money is making money. They do this by accumulating assets, and vehicles that allow money to grow. The growth of your money means more money for you. Permit yourself to have all of the money and assets you can accumulate. You deserve more money than you can count. If not you, then who? I don't just want the pie in the sky; I want the whole sky.

21

Going Forward

Release yourself from the limited thinking and boundaries you once held. As you are on this new journey, realize that you are limitless until you set a limit. Your job now as an individual accumulating wealth is to educate yourself on the tools that allow you to grow your money and assets. Learn something new and apply your knowledge. Then learn something else, and apply your expertise in that area. Now you are an asset. Use your knowledge and skills to connect with others and add value to them. Also, learn what they know and use their knowledge and skill to continue to grow yourself and your assets. Repeat the process over and over again. You are limitless, so you could never fill your mind to capacity, but you can certainly try.

Wealth Building Word: *Systematic*

Asset accumulation and management is a process that requires discipline. You could be disciplined at many things, but wealth generation requires discipline in things that bring wealth to you. Eliminating or reducing your spending on frivolous things, finding ways to produce additional income (starting a Youtube Channel or social media business page), saving, and investing are beginning points in building your wealth generation system. Make these starting points your habits, and grow yourself from there. You are limitless.

Day 7: Take Responsibility For Your Actions

When you talk and act recklessly, stand up and take owner-ship of your behavior. If you want to be celebrated for your achievements, understand that you must take responsibility for your failures. Even if no one taught you appropriate finan-cial behavior as a child, nothing stops you from learning as an adult. Absolutely nothing. Only you know your entire situation financially and in every other area of your life. No one can tell your story as well as you can, so don't expect others to know and understand. I say that meaning that you can't expect to be handled gently or for others to ignore the damage you have caused in your life and, as a result, in the lives of those around you. Your refusal to acknowledge and deal with what is ailing you mentally, physically, spiritually, etc., does not stop the damaging residue from spilling into your life. Ignoring the facts does not change the facts.

Going Forward

Deal with you. Sit down and listen to you. Examine your atti-tude, your mood swings, and your emotional state. Be honest because everything is at stake. Write down what comes to you during this time of reflection. Then take action. Talk to a trusted friend or advisor who will hold you accountable for getting to the healthiest, happiest, most lovable you. Seek professional help where it is needed. If you determine that spiritual help is what you need, get it. Do all you must do to get to the best possible you. Your first and best investment will always be...you.

Wealth Building Word: *Equilibrium*

All investors need to know that markets go up and markets go down. Movement too far up is not healthy for the market over a long period. Movement too far down is also not good for the market over a long time. After periods of extended movement in one direction or the other, the market corrects. Correction, in this case, means that the market turns from overextended in one direction and moves back in the opposite direction bringing balance or equilibrium to itself.

Day 8: You Should Be Wealthy

Wealth is not just about money. Yes, I said wealth is not just about money. Wealth could be described as the combination of everything good converging upon and spilling over in your life seemingly all at once. There is no limit to true wealth once you have it. You don't have to hurry up and live your best life now. The entirety of your life is the best when you understand that wealth is about more than the accumulation of dollars. Just as poverty permeates every aspect of a person's life, so does wealthy living.

I've heard it said over and over again that it is very expensive to be poor. I sum that up to mean poverty is a robber and a thief. How could something take away from those that have the least? As I've stated before, wealth and poverty are more than an abundance or a lack of money. Wealth, just like poverty, is a state of mind. If you believe you are poor and that's just how it will be, then guess what...you are correct. If you believe you are wealthy and that is just how it will be, then guess what...you are correct.

Going Forward

You can be wealthy, and you should be wealthy. Those are the facts. No one can deny you this privilege. Fix your mind on the idea and go do the work. You should be researching and studying wealthy people. You should be reading books by and about wealthy people. You should be acquiring skills to build your business around. You should join social media groups and chats that center around the new direction that you desire to go in. Saturate your environment and social media time with information from individuals and sources that support your new life. Doing what you have done got you this far, but the old you is not who you want to continue to be. Do something new every day. Build your new life. You deserve it.

Wealth Building Word: *Commitment*

All investing requires your commitment to being patient and sometimes fearless. All investors experience loss at one time or another. What is important is that you commit to your long-term and short-term success. Don't waver, but be singularly focused on your target. Also, commit to limiting your risk by doing your due diligence. Learn as much as you can about your investments of choice. Consult professionals where necessary. Learn, learn, learn. Execute, execute, execute. You will thank yourself later.

Day 9: Time Thief #1

I have to talk about this matter because this thief steals time from most of us because we lack discipline. I'm talking about your TV. This crafty thing is robbing many of us of the life we could be living. It robs us of time spent with family and friends. It robs children of the opportunity to engage with their parents. It causes parents to miss opportunities to build a better life for their children. TV, in the way we traditionally use it, does not benefit the everyday person.

If we are honest with ourselves, TV has raised a generation of children and changed our values. Children are in one room watching their favorite programs. The parents are in another room watching their favorite shows, and nobody interacts. The only time some families interact is when something is wrong. While everyone is entertained, no one gains anything that will help secure the family financially, emotionally, spiritually, or in any other manner. Your family needs to be secure to build a better future.

Hello...Hello...Hello...Your current skill level will likely not be enough on the scale for a highly successful existence in this coming age. I don't know if you have noticed, but Artificial Intelligence is taking over and replacing people for available jobs. Have you noticed how hard it is to get a real person on the line when you call a business? While you wasted 8 to 9 hours being entertained in front of a TV screen, you were wasting time, your most precious asset. With most people engrossed in entertainment, the world changed. Notice that

I didn't say the world is changing, but I said it has changed. The world progressed. Did you?

Going Forward

Turn off the TV. Seriously. Turn it off. You and your children do not need constant entertainment. Schedule designated time to watch TV. Turn it on during the scheduled time. Watch your show, and then turn it off again. Get into books. Take courses. Pick something that will enhance your life and cause you to move up in pay grade. You want to get away from income into cash flow, profit, and dividends. If you turn off your TV or use it to watch programming that aligns with your goals, you will eventually be in the realm of cash flow, profit, and dividends. Your mind was created to be active and innovative. Put your mind, hands, and feet to good creative use. They are waiting for you.

Wealth Building Word: *Cash flow*

Cash flow is money that comes to you from your assets. You do not have to work for this money once you acquire your assets. For example, you buy a duplex and rent out both units. One unit pays enough to cover your mortgage and expenses on the entire duplex. The other unit's rent money goes to you as money above and beyond your costs. This money will come to you as long as you own the property and it is rented out. You do not have to work for this money. That, my friend, is cash flow.

Day 10: Alignment

You say you want to be thin but don't exercise or eat right. You say you want to get to bed earlier, but neither you nor your children have a bedtime. You say you want a better job but lack new skills. You say you want to save money but will not even put away $5 per pay period or $100 when you get your tax refund. You say you want to learn how to invest, but you will not do as much as look up a free YouTube video on investing. You say many things, but your actions rarely line up with your words. Only you can change that for yourself and your impressionable children.

I mention the children because they hear you when you think they don't. They see you when you think they are not looking. They are soaking up everything you do. Your children are absorbing all of your energy. They will duplicate your efforts. Some may surpass you, but most will be right where you are right now, so take a focused look. Do you like what you see? Do you want your children in your situation, or do you want better for them? If you want a jolt, look at your parents and the things they mentioned but never saw in their lives. Look at your friends and close relatives. How many of their lives resemble the lives of their parents and close relatives? These are things to think about. If you want better, the only thing that makes sense is to get up and DO BETTER!

Going Forward

Think about your dreams—the dreams you haven't seen yet in your life. Write them down and read them out loud every day. Research what it will take for you to accomplish each of your goals, and begin to take the necessary steps. Your dreams are waiting for you. Get around people who are successful and who are constantly working towards something. You will find that the more you accomplish, the more you want to accomplish. Also, watch videos and read books that show you over and over again all the things you dream about. This will cause your dreams to grow in your mind and spirit to the point where they become a part of you. Visualizing is a way to align your reality with your words and thoughts.

Wealth Building Word: *Mutual Funds*

A mutual fund is just what the name implies. It is a pool of funds invested by a fund manager on behalf of many different investors. Investments could include stocks, bonds, real estate, short-term debts, etc. Because mutual funds are investments in many different assets, they offer instant diversification. When you invest in a mutual fund, you buy a fund's shares (parts).

Day 11: Rid Yourself and Your Family of That Selfish Thinking

As a life insurance agent, I often heard potential clients tell me that they didn't want to leave a lot of money to anybody. That was so puzzling to me. I was in my early 20s, so it caught me off guard. I thought the older generation was supposed to want better for the next generation. In my mind, I would think, how could they not want to leave the people they love in a better position?

The very same people that you spent most of your life with will have problems when you are gone. Most of their problems will come from your funeral expenses if you don't have life insurance. The loss of your income will affect the household when you are no longer there to carry or supplement the family's regular expenses. Your absence will burden your family emotionally and financially if you do not prepare properly.

Going Forward

I spoke about your final expenses earlier but go deeper than that. Break the back of lack and not enough in your family. Also, prepare to live a good life. Teach your family how to live a comfortable life without spending all they have. This will take building businesses to bring more money into the household. You will also need to learn how to invest and manage what you have. The goal is always to get to a point where you are not working for money, but your money is working for you. If you accomplish these few things in your lifetime, you have truly left your family in a better state. You will have given them tools, skills, and resources to bring money to your family as long as they stick to the principles. You will have built an invaluable legacy.

Wealth Building Word: *Producer*

A producer, in this case, is a person who makes or manufactures something. You can find a need in your community or the world and meet that need for others. In return, you receive money while solving a problem for others. Others who use your product or service are consumers. Let's use farmers as a real-world example. Farmers (producers) grow corn to keep the rest of us from being hungry. They are meeting the world's need for food. We buy the corn produced by farmers.

Day 12: Late Fees! Whyyyyy?

I cannot tell you the number of times someone (meaning well) has advised me not to pay a bill in full. Yes, you heard me correctly. They said not to pay a bill in full because that was a way for me to have some money. I wish I could explain to you how furious that made me. I hate to give my money away. I mean, I detest it, especially on things that bring no benefit to me. Paying a late fee is giving your money away.

I understand that everyone may not have all of the money they need all the time. That is what we are working on, though. We are making ourselves aware of the problems that plague us and the people around us. Paying these late fees is a problem we need to be mindful of.

Some people pay bills late simply because they are so unorganized. They lose the bill or forget it came in their email and don't think about it again until the next notice comes to them.

Get it in your head now that your bills need to be paid in full and on time every billing cycle. When the bill collector says the payment is due, it is due at that time. Pay the bill! There is no shame in doing the right thing. Anyone who tells you differently may be sincere, but their sincerity, in this case, doesn't make sense.

Going Forward

Do better than your best to pay every bill on time or pay early. If you have the money, take care of your priorities to avoid paying unnecessary fees. If you do not have the money when the bill is due, call ahead and set up payment arrangements. Be sure to stick to the payment arrangements. Also, look for a second job or side hustle to get you through the rough spots. Then take the extra money and use it to invest. This money is not for shopping, partying, or eating out. The extra money is to pay your bills so you can invest in stocks, real estate and start your business.

Wealth Building Word: *Capital*

Capital is the money you have to invest. If you have $500, $1000, $10,000, or even $100,000 to invest, that is your capital. Leave this money alone. It is not for a rainy day. That should be a separate account of money. Do not pinch off of your capital. Your capital is to be invested and left alone for the long haul. You are building generational wealth.

Day 13: Delayed Does Not Mean Denied

Many of us want everything like yesterday. Today is too late. It coulda, woulda, shoulda been mine yesterday. Stop the foolishness. Seriously. If your grandparents were not wealthy, your parents were more than likely not wealthy. Which leads us right to you. You are probably not wealthy at this point, either. Therefore, stop thinking you will get wealthy in one night. You may get wealthy overnight, but it won't be in one night. It may take many long nights. It may take many long days also, but your job is not to worry about what is not happening. Your job is to set goals that will lead to your desired outcome. If being a multi-thousandaire or multi-millionaire is your desire, keep taking steps in that direction. If your goal is just to leave something for your children, keep taking steps in that direction. Just because nothing appears to be happening doesn't mean nothing is happening. If you are putting in the effort, then something is happening. It takes just as much work and effort to be poor as it does to be rich. Think about that. You make time for what you want now, but it does not lead you to your dream of wealth. Take that same energy to build your business, learn a new skill, or learn about investing. How quickly something happens is not the most important thing. The most important thing is that you start and never give up. If you get going and keep going, you will be successful.

Going Forward

You can wait. You don't need to see everything happening. Take your time. Take the steps you have outlined through your research or your mentor. You are doing things differently. You are thinking differently. Things will happen for you because you are working for what you want. A delay, a minor setback, or a misstep can't take you off your course. Only you can do that, but you will not. Understand now that you are doing a good thing and that greatness is your destiny. It cannot be denied.

Wealth Building Word: *Timing*

Timing is key. You cannot go ahead of where you should be. You have to learn all of your lessons. You cannot be a step behind where you should be. You are only delaying yourself. Things will happen when they are supposed to happen. Just be ready.

Day 14: Fear

People, People, People. Listen. Scared money does not make money. Seriously though. Stop being so frightened of losing what you have that you never get in the game. If the outcome of investing was so bad, why do the opportunities still exist? Why do people still learn about the stock market? Why do people have whole careers in and around the investment markets? Wake up and stop the madness. Your fear has kept you on the sidelines long enough. Get in the game. Don't only get in the game; GO WIN! People are winning in the markets every single day. Every day of your life, someone is winning in the markets, whether it's the stock market, the foreign exchange market, the cryptocurrency market, the real estate market, etc. People are winning in this information and technological age at a rate unlike any other. If you are stuck in fear, you are falling behind. There is no such thing as standing still. You are either falling behind or moving ahead. Get going!!!

Going Forward

Get yourself educated on whatever you desire to pursue. Do not try to be a hero immediately out of the gate, but take some time to get informed. Many people lose because they didn't take the time to properly educate themselves beforehand. I am not necessarily talking about going to college if that is not your thing. I am saying - learn from this information age we are in. You have access to cellphones and computers; put them to work on your behalf. Do the research. Put in the hours, and you will see results. Search for a particular interest group on social media, and you will be surprised by what comes up. Jump in and start asking questions. Someone will comment, even if it is not the person that made the video or account. Participation in anything says that you will lose something (more than likely your old self) at some point. Nonparticipation also guarantees a loss. You lose the opportunity to win, so go play. Get in the game. With time, patience, and skill development, you will win at whatever you set your mind to accomplish.

Wealth Building Word: *Risk*

All investing involves risk, which simply means you could lose all or part of your investment. I would rather work my way back from a $300 out of $1,000 loss than go to a mall and spend $1,000 on consumable items (name-brand clothes, shoes, jewelry, etc.) that will likely be out of style next year. The remaining $700 is still a seed of opportunity.

Day 15: Tax Refund

This topic is something that burns a hole in my soul. Many people get a tax refund every year. Many of these same people receive $10,000, $12,000, or $15,000 per year. Unfortunately, all that money is spent each year in a month or two. I mean spent. Gone. Poof. Vanished. These people's lives return to normal as if they never had that windfall of money. It's back to borrowing money from family and friends. This evaporating money situation blows my mind every year. It is like a tale of two moods. In one mood, everyone is excited and sitting on top of the world when that money finally arrives. Once the money is spent, all of the joy seems to leave again.

Please understand that $10,000, $12,000, and $15,000 are not large sums of money when you look at your total life. The proof is in how fast you spend that amount of money. You had that money for a few days or weeks, then it was all gone, and you have nothing to show for it. If you had just invested some of your money each year, you would see it growing. Invested money grows like a tree. I did not say it grows on trees, but it grows like a tree...slow and steady in most cases.

Going Forward

See your refund money as a seed. The seed needs to be planted in a good investment to grow. You must educate yourself and discover your interest to determine a good investment. You have an entire year between tax refunds to research and find your way around the investment world. Find beginner's investments and work your way up. Then move on to other types of investments that fit your goals. Consuming your seed is a thing of the past for you. You got this!!!

Wealth Building Word: *Equity*

In real estate, equity is the difference between what you paid for the property and the higher market value of the property if it increases. Likewise, if a business was to liquidate and pay off all its debts, the money left over would be the equity. This money could be given to shareholders. There are also other ways to view equity, so continue to research.

Day 16: Lottery Ticket

I will try to contain myself on this one, but have you ever heard any stories about people winning the lottery and going broke? I would love to experience that kind of windfall at one time, but I wonder if I would lose my everlasting mind. The things people do with their money when they win the lottery are crazy to me. Buying multi-million dollar houses, the most expensive cars, blinged-out jewelry, and vacations for the whole crew. I mean, people go crazy and try to live their best life all in a short period of time.

On the other hand, some people get depressed because they can't handle the pressure of dealing with family and friends coming out of the woodwork, asking for money and just wanting to be around them all the time. The depression also comes from deep-seated issues that they've had buried all along. I heard a saying that money doesn't necessarily change you, but it makes you more of who you are.

If you were reckless and careless before you had money, you will likely be more of that person with money. If you were unhappy most of the time before you had money, you would likely be an unhappy camper with all of your money. My point in saying all of this is to say you need a plan. Since you plan to have millions or billions of dollars, start to plan for it now. I know it sounds unbelievable, but I am 100% serious.

Going Forward

If you decide not to learn how to invest your own money, begin to look up financial planners. Also, begin to research lawyers. You will need someone to look out for you when it comes to reading and signing important documents and your business pursuits. If you are going to go big, you may need a security detail and a personal assistant. Most importantly, get professional help for what ails you mentally. You are going to need your entire mind to enjoy your best life. You don't want old heavy baggage weighing you down. Look into these things now because you are fueling your dreams. Pursuit of your goals takes action on your part. Don't just keep the steps to your dream in your head; live them out loud now.

Wealth Building Word: *Balance Sheet*

A balance sheet is where a person or a business keeps track of assets (things that grow in value and can produce an income) and liabilities (debts and possessions that depreciate). The goal is to continuously increase your assets and decrease liabilities. As you increase your number of assets and decrease your liabilities, you are growing your wealth.

Day 17: Dream Killers

If you go after your goals and dreams, be careful who you allow to be in your personal space. Some would try to tear you down to your face. Everyone knows that one person who can really just get under their skin in the worst way. Stay away from them. They take too much of your time and energy.

I am also saying stay away from that person who is a disaster waiting to happen. We have all heard stories about the good person who got caught in the wrong place at the wrong time, with the wrong people, possibly doing the wrong thing, but more than likely doing nothing at the time. Don't be this person. Choose your friends wisely. Yes, you all may have a long history, but realize that history is just that...it's the past.

The final person I want to address is the ever-so-kind person who always wants to be around you. They don't seem to do much. You are their only daily goal, but their lack of desire and drive for life irritates you. Whether you realize it or not, that person saps your energy and, in some ways, distracts you. The irritation they cause pulls away from energy that could be used for creativity and productivity. Am I saying to crush someone's heart and to treat them in a harmful way... NEVER. I am saying, take the necessary steps to protect your goals and dreams.

Going Forward

Protect your energy by limiting access to yourself to people who are not on your path. Love your family and friends, but schedule the love fest where possible. Just be sure to take time out for your goals and dreams. The more your desire for your goals and dreams grows, the more you will need to spend time working on them. Sacrifice is okay. You will be fine. They will be fine. Keep your promises to yourself and others, but remember you can't be everywhere with everyone all the time: schedule, schedule, schedule. Keep going. You can do it.

Wealth Building Word: *Investor*

An investor is not necessarily a saver. Investing and saving are two different things. Saving involves holding money that is not or is barely growing in value. An investor is a person who buys assets: stocks, bonds, real estate, businesses, precious metals, etc. An investor fully expects their money to grow as a result of being invested. Invested capital has an assignment to produce something (usually more money or value), whereas saved money is simply expected to be there.

Day 18: Surround Yourself with Greatness

You must be careful to be around people who are going somewhere in life. Always being around people doing the same things they were doing 5, 10, 15, or 20 years ago may not be in your best interest. The things you have done are the things that have gotten you as far as you are today. If you are dissatisfied with today's you, you must make changes. Continuing to do the same things but expecting different results is insane. You need to be inspired to do more things that lead you to your goals. The people that surround you should be a part of that inspiration.

Once again, I am not saying to abandon your family. I suggest getting into reading books about people that inspire you. Buy the hardcover or paperback version of books because you can hold them in your hands. Buy posters or print pictures of people you admire and hang them up. Do whatever it takes to surround yourself with the greatest minds of all time and the people in your chosen field that inspire you.

Going Forward

Go buy some books. Explore people and places that you have never been interested in before. The goal is to surround yourself with the best of the best, whether they are in your chosen field or not. Greatness inspires greatness. Yes, you are great. You will also be great at what you decide to do in your business pursuits, investing style, and creative endeavors. You become what you are surrounded with. Therefore, surround yourself with greatness.

Wealth Building Word: *Company*

There are different types of business entities or companies that you can form. These entities include sole proprietors, limited liability corporations, C corporations, and S corporations. Individuals or groups form these companies to provide a service, make money, gain tax benefits, and use them to protect themselves against lawsuits. Research company types or consult a professional to determine the type of business entity you want to form for yourself when you are ready for that stage.

Day 19: Spending Plans and Budgets

We all need to track where our money is going, but very few people do this. You need money to advance through the different stages of being an investor. You have money coming in, so spend it wisely. Know where your money is going. Some people prefer budgets or ways of allocating money to certain things. I prefer my idea of a spending plan for everything that needs to be paid.

In my spending plan, I list everything down to the smallest detail, including my giving and bills as low as $3 per month. This is important because I always know where I stand with my money. I know even before I get paid, especially since my pay and expenses remain close to the same from one month to the next. Doing this allows me to quickly and efficiently ensure everything is paid on time. I write due dates in my spending plan also.

Recurring essential bills are automatically deducted from my account to ensure they are paid on time. For expenses that are not essential but add to my life in some way, I sit down and pay them monthly. I can call and cancel them at any time, though. Doing things this way protects me from paying late fees and other unnecessary expenses. I know what I am expected to pay every month, and I pay it on time or before it is due.

Going Forward

Make your spending plan or budget. You are growing and going to new heights in your life, so you must do things differently. You are taking control of your life and finances, so you can make your dreams, vision, and goals a reality. Some people will require professional help, so get it. Others will do the research and get the job done on their own. Whatever your approach is, do not delay or skip this step. If money gets tight for you, you don't want to go into your investments, so make your plan now. Planning is a vital present step towards you getting to your long-term goals.

Wealth Building Word: *Price versus Cost*

Many consumers look at price as being the cost of something. Investors know there is more to price than just the cost of something. Price is the amount someone is willing to pay for something. Cost is the amount paid by a manufacturer to produce something. The price of assets changes all the time based on market conditions. Supply and demand are factors that influence price. Demand or possible scarcity of products or services could increase prices. When in business, the price is expected to exceed the cost to make a profit.

Day 20: Stop Spending All of Your Money

I already know your money is your money. I also already know that you are an adult and can spend as much of your money as possible. However, I am going to tell you as a friend...STOP SPENDING ALL OF YOUR MONEY. I am so serious. You should always have some money. Some people don't even have $5 left over between paychecks. If you are spending all your money, you must determine why. Something should always be left over for you.

I don't know what it is, but I have seen people not satisfied until every penny is spent, even if they have everything they need at the time. It is like they have a severe hate relationship with money. Almost as if they don't want money around them.

Then some get paid every Thursday or Friday, and the money is totally gone by Monday. All they did was party all weekend. Then they have to pay the money back to everyone they borrowed from to make it to the next paycheck. Once the next check comes, the spending starts all over again.

Some people treat spending like a drug. They don't feel right if they are not spending money. They get a sort of high from spending. Wake up and realize that the down and depressed mood happens because you have spent all your money, and now you don't have any. You borrow, and that probably makes you feel bad. Now you have just enough to make it to your next paycheck. Payday comes, and your high returns again - not off of drugs but off of the opportunity to spend more money.

It is okay to have money. Hear me; it is okay for you to have money in the bank, in your pocket, under the mattress, or in a pillowcase. Just make sure you have some money left over somewhere, please.

Going Forward

Set aside a day or two per week where you do not spend any money. Once you pick your day or two, stick to your plan. The key is to be consistent. Not spending on Wednesday does not mean you can break the bank on Thursday. Take the money you did not spend and put it towards your emergency fund, or buy a share of stock. If you don't have a plan for your money, make one, and stick to it. The more consistent you are, the better your results will be. Get comfortable with the idea of having money just because it is possible.

Wealth Building Word: *Appreciation*

Appreciation can be explained as showing growth. When a stock appreciates, that means it increases in value. If the stock was $110 this year, but it is worth $121 next year, it has appreciated in value.

Day 21: Needless Things

I am about to say something really important right here. People may think I am crazy, but I will say it anyway...STOP HAVING HUGE 1-YEAR-OLD BIRTHDAY EXTRAVAGANZAS. I am so serious. The baby is barely conscious of the world, and the family is going all out throwing the party of the year. Why? A huge party for a 1-year-old winds up being an adult party. Why go through the trouble of hats, balloons, parting gifts, decorations, cakes, cupcakes, macaroni and cheese, shrimp, crabs, fried chicken, ribs, a DJ, etc.? Why do all of that in the name of the baby barely aware of anything? Am I saying not to celebrate? No, I am not. Watch what you are spending. I used the example of a party for a 1-year-old, but the idea is the same for whatever needless things you do (gender reveal party, etc.). Stop using your money for temporary pleasures or to impress other people. Put your money into things with lasting value.

Going Forward

Ask yourself when you get ready to spend money if the thing you are buying is needless or necessary. If you are honest with yourself, you will find that many purchases are needless. As I stated before, many things could be considered unnecessary, but to refer back to the 1-year-old having a birthday extravaganza, what if you requested instead of giving gifts that whoever wanted to give something send money to a Cash App account? Once all funds are received, purchase a stock, bond, or mutual fund for the child's benefit.

The party will not be remembered, but that needful purchase of stocks, bonds, or mutual funds will be around for a very long time. Now you have something to show the child as they grow, and hopefully, spark a flame towards financial literacy and responsibility.

Wealth Building Word: *Depreciation*
Depreciation is when something loses value. You pay one price for a car at the dealership. As soon as you drive off in the car, it begins to lose value. The car is worth less and less the more you drive it. A car for your personal use is not an asset. Assets increase in value over time and have the potential to produce cash flow.

Day 22: Fear of Missing Out, Otherwise Known As FOMO

We fear many things, but my focus here is not really on the fear that paralyzes us and causes us not to act when we should. I'm talking about the exact opposite. The dumb stuff we do. Yes, I said the dumb stuff. I'm talking about the dumb stuff like giving your cousin money for a business that will make you a million dollars by next week. Even more dumb stuff like trusting a stranger with large sums of money they promise will bring you all of your dreams and desires. STOP IT! Look carefully at your situation. Find what you don't like, and ask yourself, how long did it take for things to get to where they are now? Ask yourself that question, pause, and give yourself an honest response.

Understand that your situation is not how it is because of one night. Your situation is the way it is because of many small steps day after day and night after night. Whether conscious or unconscious, you built your life to be how it is over time. Just as it was built over time, it will need to be fixed over time. The main thing is identifying the problem and acknowledging that it needs to be fixed. The fact that you would give your hard-earned money to someone promising the miraculous says that you want to change, so be about the change. Get yourself educated on finances and investing.

Learn, learn, learn. There are many ways to earn money, but you must ask yourself which is for you.

Going Forward

Be willing to put in the work. Also, understand that you should not skip any steps. Take your bumps and bruises like a champ and get up and win. You've been winning, so don't let a quick fix make you lose your mind. Discipline and patience have gotten you this far. Stick to the new habits you have learned. Walk with the understanding that some things will happen quickly and others will happen at a snail's pace. You are not worried about any of that. Your concern is preparing every day. Take one step and then the next step toward your goals, dreams, and desires. Lose that fear and be bold.

Wealth Building Word: *Wall Street Journal*

Read, read, read! Once again, read. Pick up the Wall Street Journal and read it. The Wall Street Journal is a newspaper that focuses on business. It still comes in paper format but can also be found online. Most people with big money read the Wall Street Journal every day. People aspiring to have big money should do what people with money do. Make it a habit. You can download the app or even get it through Apple News+ for a monthly fee. Watching TV your whole life is played out. Do a new thing...read and learn about money and business. Then get you some business and money.

Day 23: Have Stuff Without Stuff Having You

Too often, we consume, consume, consume. We consume with no thought given to the future. And I'm not even talking about the distant future; I'm talking about a month or two down the road. We often jump for the quick fix, but we must realize that the long game is the way to go. Running to spend money on new clothes, shoes, cars, and jewelry doesn't show a return. Most of those things are useless once you possess them. They do not offer you one ray of hope for the future, but you want it anyway. You want it, and you have to have it right away. How do you feel once you get whatever you had to have right away? At first, you may stare at your new stuff. You wear it or drive it around and love that all eyes are on you. After all of that, how do you feel?

Those that sit and reflect may have some buyer's remorse. They may feel sick to their stomach even. They may even tell themselves they need to get out of debt and put some money away. Some people may or may not start to do just that. Then some don't give themselves time to reflect. They are off to get more money to buy more things to feel good again. These people may only consider saving or investing when someone mentions it. These people may think saving and investing are for others and that they could never learn to do either. They just continue consuming everything they get because it makes them feel good. This is a case of stuff having you.

Going Forward

Set a structure for yourself. Agree with yourself to set aside a certain amount of money to invest each month. This is not savings account money. This is investment account money. Saving and investing are two separate things. You want to build yourself up to do both. You determine how you will split your money between your accounts, but be sure to be building both at all times. Having and executing a plan for yourself will guide you toward the discipline you need to accomplish your financial goals.

Wealth Building Word: *Brokerage*

A brokerage is like a bank, but you go to the brokerage to buy stocks, ETFs, bonds, and other financial instruments and services. Some brokerages offer banking services with really decent rates. Do your research and see which will fit your investing and banking needs.

Day 24: What Good Are Your Shoulders If No One Can Stand On Them?

Being a pillar of strength and hope for your family and community should be priority number 1 for every individual. Your goal should be to always be your best because so many eyes are on you. All eyes are on you. Your family sees you. They look to you, so what will you do with this responsibility? Will you accept it, or will you run in the other direction? That is something we all have to ask ourselves. When you ask yourself, answer honestly.

Whatever you decide will require commitment. Picking up the responsibility will require you to be something you haven't been before, and not picking up the commitment will also require you to be something you haven't been before. You've never been a quitter, so don't start now.

Pick yourself up from your setbacks and continue to run your race. Your race is a marathon that seems like it will never end, but that is okay. You're not concerned with the end because you don't have control over that. Your concern is running because you have absolute control over that. You'll grow and evolve along the way. The things you thought you couldn't handle make you want to reach the end that much faster, but they are building you up. You'll run your race with grace and strength, but you must commit. You are irreplaceable in your marathon. There is no substitute for you.

Going Forward

See yourself as the seed that has to grow into a beautiful tree for your entire family to eat from. You are the investment. What you do with yourself will be the building block for those who come after you. They'll stand as high as you can lift them. You're not worried about what things look like because everything may not be right. You are running your race with a clear vision of where you are going, and you will take the people who will work hard and who desire to go with you. You will not take those that hinder you, but those that will grow with you and even exceed you. You are the seed for someone else's harvest. Your shoulders will solidly hold your loved ones.

Wealth Building Word: *Solid*

When you start to invest, you don't want to just go with any company that another person suggested. You want to invest in solid companies. Solid, in this instance, means a company with income statements, balance sheets, and cash flow statements that meet your criteria. You will have to do research or get with someone or a company to help you learn what to look for in a company. There are different methods for evaluating companies, but research and determine what works best for you. YouTube is a good starting place. Watch various videos and make comparisons to find out what is important to you when evaluating a company. When you learn, teach someone else.

Day 25: Life Insurance

Life insurance is a topic that needs to be addressed in a candid and sincere way. Think about it. You have plans to become an investor and to be filthy rich. If you or a family member passed away suddenly, would you be prepared, or would you have to liquidate your savings and investments to bury your loved one or yourself? This is a serious question. You should give it some thought. I know GoFundMe is an option, but do you want to do that to bury your loved one? I think not. Life insurance is important in building and protecting the wealth and legacy you desire to build for your family.

Life insurance not only protects you if a loved one passes away but is also a way to pass down wealth to your family.

Some people acquire whole life insurance because it builds a cash value you could borrow against and use if needed. Whole life insurance is more expensive. There is also term insurance that is usually less expensive and allows you to purchase more insurance.

One key thing to remember is that the money still needs to be managed properly to provide for the family for the long haul. Learning about investing and teaching your children to invest will help them to take care of the money instead of spending on frivolous things until it all runs out. You'll secure your legacy as you learn and take the proper steps to do the right things. You will ensure that your descendants

97

will never have to endure some of the things you did because you laid a solid foundation.

Going Forward

Change your mindset. You are an investor now. You are always looking for ways and opportunities to invest. You protect your assets, and you decrease and eliminate liabilities. You protect what you have built for the long haul. You are contacting an insurance agent and getting you and everyone you are responsible for covered. You are eliminating as many setbacks as possible. Your family will be secure because of your efforts to care for them. They will get it. Everything that you are trying to teach will sink in. You just keep going.

Wealth Building Word: *Passive Income*

Truly wealthy people do not work for money. Most wealthy people do things they enjoy for a living. The hard work has already been done, and they are enjoying the benefits of the work they or someone in their family already did. Whatever the work was or the investment that took place, they continued to get paid for it. That is passive income. Money that keeps coming whether you do anything else or not. For example, owning a property and renting it out creates passive income. Your money will continue to flow as long as you own the property and have it rented out.

Day 26: SHOW UP!

I know we all miss the mark occasionally, but for the most part, we can be on point most of the time. It boils down to a decision to do the right thing in as many moments as possible. We can't talk about money without talking about the whole person. Money will not necessarily make you a new person, but it will make you more of the person you were on the inside all along.

If you were a dirty rotten scoundrel before you had money, more than likely, you'd take the dirty rotten scoundrel to new heights after you get money. If you were a kind, loving person before you had money, you'd certainly continue in that vein after you acquire your fortune. I'm not locking anyone into a specific destiny but do the research. You could probably look around you and see how possessions didn't change who a person was on the inside, but possessions may have made them more of who they were already.

My point in saying "SHOW UP!" is to work on being your best self now. Don't wait until you have it all. You don't know what that life holds for you, but you know where you are. Be present with you. Be real with you. Challenge yourself to go forward in every aspect of your life: body, soul, and spirit.

Going Forward

Be honest with yourself and identify your weaknesses. Write them down so that you can look at them repeatedly. You're not looking at them to rehearse how bad of a person you are. You are looking at them and picking an area to focus your energy and effort on correcting. Some of your weaknesses will overlap, and that is okay. All of life intertwines. Other shortcomings may take a long time to adjust. The point is to work on being the best you. There is no time limit. This is not a sprint. Your lifework is a marathon. In a marathon, the runners get started, and some wonder when the end will come while others run strong all the way. The thing they have in common is that they all started. They got in the race, and so will you. You are your biggest and best investment. You will rise to the occasion. You will "SHOW UP!".

Wealth Building Word: *Going Long*

When trading, traders can take a position, based on analysis, for the market to go up, or long. If your position was long and the market did go up and hit your target, as you had hoped, then you had a winning trade. Investors buy stocks, mutual funds, bonds, and other securities with the hopes that the market will go long/up, thereby increasing the value of their security.

Day 27: Your Attitude

Even when investing, you have to have the right attitude, or things will not work in your favor because the negativity will blind you. It's almost as if you're throwing a blanket over your own head, blocking your eyes, and going for a walk. Your intention is to see, but you've given your energy over to something that causes you not to see. Negativity blocks not only your physical sight but also your vision. Your vision is what you can imagine and dream about before it even happens. If you are the dam that is blocking your own vision from coming to pass, that will be reflected in your attitude. That dam of negativity prevents your dreams and vision from flowing to bring you your highest aspirations.

Going Forward

Remove the covering from your own eyes, or get help. Find a trusted friend or mentor to help you in your journey to your highest aspirations. Your mentor or trusted friend should be able to see things you may have overlooked about yourself. Hopefully, the mentor or trusted friend you choose to walk with you on this journey will have experienced the heights you desire to attain. They can make you aware of pitfalls and educate you along the way. Connect and feed off of each other's energy.

Trust the process. Do what you are told. Take every challenge and smash it even if you're afraid. If you're afraid, keep taking the challenge...every time. Do not let a negative attitude dictate how you interact with the people helping you. Show them respect, and appreciate them for helping you. This is all about you being your best, but you need help. Accept the help.

Wealth Building Word: *Bullish*

Markets have different sentiments. When you hear the term bullish, it means the market is expected to go up (higher). The market can go upward from a low position. It can even continue to go up from an elevated position. A market moving upwards has a bullish sentiment.

Day 28: Stank Thinking

If you believe you can change your life, guess what? You can. You absolutely can change your financial future also. You can change your educational future. You can change your spiritual future. You can change your marital future. You are in absolute control of what you do. Why do I say that? Because everything starts with a decision.

Your new you. Your brighter future. Everything you hope to accomplish starts today with you making a decision and acting on it. Please don't confuse this one-time decision with the result. Your decision today will have to be followed by another decision in the same direction tomorrow and day after day until you reach your desired goal.

You will try to get in your way. Make no doubt about that. You will more than likely be your worst enemy and critic. Push you out of your way like a bad habit. Every day will not be the best of days. Some days will be the worst of days. You will fail. You will resort to old methods of comforting yourself on your journey, but rest assured that you are not the same person. You have come too far. You will never again rest in any state other than the state of being your highest self. You have evolved. You are new. In some circles, you are unrecognizable because you took a chance on yourself. What others thought about you and what you thought about yourself that didn't align with your higher purpose will never rule in your life again. You are now free.

Going Forward

Affirm your new self every day. Write a declaration that you say to yourself out loud every day. It can be a list, or it could be one thing that you say repeatedly. Investing and trading are more about your thinking than technical and fundamental analysis. You could observe everything correctly on the screen but talk yourself out of your trade because your internal thinking is off. You may think you have no right to win. You may think you have no right to prosper. Stop it! You have every right to win. You have every right to prosper. I already told you you have evolved. You are new. Now make your list and say it out loud every day until you believe. Add to the list when necessary. You can never say enough great things about yourself. You are no longer caught up in stank thinking. Your thoughts are of peace, wealth, and prosperity.

Wealth Building Word: *Options*

When trading, you have the opportunity to buy shares of stocks outright. You can also make a down payment (premium) on a certain number of shares. This is called an Option. The down payment (premium) is usually non-refundable, but it allows you the right to buy the number of shares you paid the premium on at a later date if you decide to purchase them. You also have the choice to sell your rights to these shares of stock once you've paid your premium on them. This is all handled through a contract, which is handled through a broker. Do more research on options.

Day 29: Financially Literate is Still Basically Poor

Yep! Let that marinate. Simply knowing a whole lot of stuff doesn't make you rich. Being the smartest in your circle doesn't equate to money in your pockets either. What you do with your knowledge and money is more important than simply knowing a few things.

Standing around bragging but never getting into the markets is useless. You are wasting time and energy gaining knowledge if you don't even have a brokerage account. Learning to have a budget or a spending plan are basic things. Getting your credit in order only allows you to borrow more money from truly wealthy people. Knowing how to get a mortgage is also a basic thing.

You can tell what the basic things are because those are the things that you learn in school. You can learn all of those things at free seminars. Taking care of basic things does help you to reduce stress and to keep order in your life concerning finances, but they do not elevate you to the level of someone acquiring wealth and freedom. Truly wealthy people have businesses and assets that pay them repeatedly. Their focus is on acquiring more assets to continue the wealth-building process. If you pay attention, every presidential candidate promises to tax the rich. Why is taxing the rich always a campaign promise? Why aren't the rich taxed like any other hard-working person? The rich understand how money works. Their money does not just sit in a bank account. Their money is working for them to bring in more money. Truly wealthy people can leave a legacy for their descendants, and it is their pleasure to do so.

Going Forward

You are getting yourself solid on the basic things like good credit, budgeting, saving, primary home buying, etc. You are focusing your energy on investing, business building, and networking. You should also be examining who in your circle is with you. You will have to spend less time with the people who aspire to keep the same thing the main thing because you are aspiring to a life of abundance for yourself and your family. That is your focus. A wealthy family must come from you. That will take your time, your energy, and your focus. You can only carry those willing to at least be helpful on your journey. Most of your time, space, and energy are for things that prosper you.

Wealth Building Word: *Leverage*

Using other people's money to invest instead of using your own money is called leverage. An example of this is obtaining a mortgage to buy a home. Most people don't have the money to pay for a home outright, so they get leverage (a loan) to buy the house. Keep in mind that loans have interest charges. That means keeping your credit score in the 670 and above range because you do not want your interest rate to be too high. If the interest rate is too high, your payments will also be high, and you may not be able to pay consistently, or you will be financially strapped.

Day 30: So Wrong, You Think You're Right

Why did someone who frequently borrows money tell me that looking good is more important than having money? Why did that happen? It happened because most people need vision. Seriously. Some people are so blind in their minds that they genuinely believe that an outfit that matches in every way or a different pair of shoes every day to go with all of their outfits is living life. Wrong. You are wrong about that, and stop arguing with me about it.

Your children see what you do. They will also do what you do. It is safe to say that your children will not have money saved or invested. Your children will have to borrow money from someone to buy more time to repay someone else they owe. Your children will look nice but be filled with stress and searching for relief. Is that what you want? Giving your children the things you didn't have as a child can be done, but you have to see beyond today. That stress you feel is not normal. It may be common, but it is not normal.

Going Forward

Hopefully, you're so mad at yourself that you will open your eyes and make a change for the next generation. Your changes starting today and carried out as life changes will impact your family for generations. Decide to cut down on your spending. See your financial situation as undesirable, and change it. Take the money you save from buying one less pair of shoes, and invest it in something that interests you. You could buy a stock, a book, a course, or a seminar. Get out of the wrong way of thinking and acting. Do the right thing, and be right. Take a balanced approach and invest. Don't just consume. Invest.

Wealth Building Word: *Resistance*

When the market rises from a lower level and gets to a point/ level that it has trouble breaking through, that is called resistance. The market will often reverse and go back down to lower levels at this point. Sometimes the market breaks through this tough spot after several failed attempts. Even after breaking up through resistance, the market can be drawn back to a point of former resistance.

Day 31: Setbacks Shouldn't Make You Quit

Time out for quitting. Quit shouldn't even be in your vocabulary anymore. You are doing this. You are 100% dedicated and committed to your success as an investor, trader, researcher, writer, or anything you set your heart and mind to be. You are that. No more starting and stopping. You've seen that enough in your life. Think about all the times your parents told you they would do something. Think about all the times you've seen them fail. You witnessed your hero's failure. Think about that. This larger-than-life figure in your life failed. They may or may not have disappointed you in their failure, but you learned that failure is possible. It didn't change the fact that you were looking up to them. Yes, your eyes and heart were as fixed as ever on what your parents would provide for you. Know that someone is looking at you in the same way. I'm asking you to change the game, though. Rewrite the narrative.

Change the game if you were without because of your parent's shortcomings and lack of knowledge. Go for more. Build and leave a legacy. Provide a rich heritage for your family. Dig in now so that the make-up of your family is so different that people who knew you all before have to come to know you again. Don't look like your past. That's behind you. Wealth, riches, and opportunities are ever before you. Grab them all now.

Going forward

Remove the word quit from your vocabulary and thinking. Replace it with words like lesson and perseverance. Tell yourself that every loss is a lesson and that you will press on and persevere through the setback. Look at your loss or disappointment as you simply learned what doesn't work for you. You'll pick yourself up. You'll keep reading, you'll keep writing, and you'll keep looking at the data until everything makes sense to you. Then you'll continue to sharpen yourself with the understanding that your learning never ends. Your growth process will be a welcomed part of the new you when you grasp the concept of perpetual learning. There is always something to learn.

Wealth Building Word: *Analysis*

Learning the markets is an ongoing process. You can look at the stock charts and interpret what you see. You can read or listen to all of the news and analyze the information. All this contact with knowledge goes through your filter to make sense of what you heard or saw. That is your analysis. The key thing with analysis is consistency and putting all the information together to make it useful for you. Then you are on your way to being very successful.

Congratulations! You made it to the end of this book, but realize this is just a step along your journey. I hope you are forever impacted and encouraged to never stop learning and growing. If you've never given much thought to the ideas presented in these pages, then you are at the beginning; keep going. If the ideas presented here are building blocks from previous knowledge, I am glad you continued to the end, and I hope you found some gems to aid you along your path. This book is only a small piece of the puzzle. There is so much information out there and so many ways to apply it.

One last thing I want you to take with you, none of this (talking about money and broadening your understanding) is about money for the sake of flexing your possessions or keeping score with others. The true power is in the discipline and structure required from us to obtain more and utilize it most effectively. I would choose to be able to afford a safe community for my family, access to high-quality schools and stores that actually sell food that promotes healthy living vs. worrying about my child's well-being on the playground, low-quality education, and living in a food desert every time.

As you are motivated, empowered, and equipped to benefit in life, remember to teach others to do the same. Wherever you are in your journey, I wish you all the best that life has to offer. Always get your dollars and make sense. Peace.